Just A Few Things
THAT NEED TO
BE SAID

Just A Few Things THAT NEED TO BE SAID

An Ordinary American's Commentary on Today's Society

Thomas E. Gray

gatekeeper press

Columbus, Ohio

Just A Few Things That Need To Be Said: An Ordinary
American's Commentary on Today's Society

Published by Gatekeeper Press
2167 Stringtown Rd, Suite 109
Columbus, OH 43123-2989
www.GatekeeperPress.com

The editorial work for this book is entirely the product of
the author. Gatekeeper Press did not participate in and is
not responsible for any aspect of the editorial work.

Library of Congress Control Number: 2019952571
ISBN (paperback): 9781642378382
eISBN: 9781642378399

CONTENTS

PREFACE

There are just a few things that need to be said. There are so many things going on in this country that never receive attention by the elites on television. I, for once, would like to tell people what I and a lot of other people think, but are often either afraid to say, too polite to say, or are never given the opportunity to say.

I have attempted to make commentary on some more serious issues and also on some less serious issues of our times. This is not a great theological discourse on our society, but I do believe that many of the things mentioned in this book are symptoms of a decline in American culture.

Some readers will be offended. The truth often offends those who aren't interested in hearing the truth.

A lot of readers may laugh and say, "It's about time someone said what I was thinking."

CHAPTER 1

The So-called Digital Age

I sincerely believe that the so-called "digital age" is making people less intelligent over time. This over-reliance on technology is turning many people into braindead robots who can't even relate to other human beings. This over-reliance on technology is also causing people to lose their ability to think critically and to problem solve.

I LOATHE SOCIAL MEDIA!

We have bred a generation of young people who have such delusional self-importance, that they feel the need to broadcast their every thought and whim in various posts and texts about their mundane daily activities. How boring! People have become so egotistical that they feel the need to update their social media page with a photo of the cookies they just baked. I, as their friend on the media page, even receive alerts for such major updates. When we encourage people in such self-indulgent behavior, it creates a situation in which they never learn to think beyond themselves. These people are so egocentric that they now even insert themselves into other people's tragedies, for example, via a Twitter posting, and end up making the tragedy about themselves.

How do they do that… you may ask? For example, a news story appears about the death of a child or some other tragic event, involving complete strangers. We will often see a posting under the news story such as this. "My heart goes out to these poor people, and my prayers are with them." The prayers and thoughts are great things, but why broadcast it? By posting this declaration, the social media user has demonstrated again my very point. Posting about thoughts and prayers does nothing for the people involved in a tragic situation. It only serves to demonstrate an egocentric mentality by making the issue about self.

The younger generation wouldn't know the truth if it bit them. We have trained a generation of people to assume everything they read in social media is the "truth" when it often is far from the truth. We now see the younger generation of journalists sharing news stories based on some random person's Twitter posting, which is usually self-absorbed and hardly objective. This is very dangerous. Basing news stories on social media posts often creates news stories that are based completely on emotions and rarely upon truth. We see people adamantly claiming someone said this or that, when they have never even listened personally to the person they are quoting. What they end up quoting is what someone else has said someone else said or did. This is very dangerous.

Why do I continue to focus on truth, people may ask? The truth is fundamental to our survival as a nation. When truth no longer matters in our most basic mundane lives, how can we expect the truth to prevail when attempting to solve the most critical issues that involve our nation? The lack of truth results in the lack of educated and forthright debate in our public forums, such as even among our very own United States Congress.

TECHNOLOGY IS GREAT BUT IT IS RUINING PEOPLE.

How can I say such a thing? I see it every day. Young people can't even spell simple words, and they certainly don't know much about what it means to read a book. Over-reliance on technology and social media postings to obtain information has resulted in profound falsehoods to be perpetuated and believed by many. These so-called "connected" people are the most disconnected people I know. They have deluded themselves into thinking they have hundreds of friends.

I ask any of these people the following, "How many of these social media friends are going to show up when your parents die? How many of them are going to show up and loan you money when you experience hard times? How many of them are going to be at your very own funeral? Let me be straight with you: if your answer is 'No' to any or all of these three basic questions, then they are not your friends."

Young people are delusional about what it means to be a friend. They have turned one of the most basic and valued aspects of life a person can possess into cheap and lazy efforts, disguised as friendship. No longer are people expected to demonstrate true loyalty and friendship. Instead, they are allowed to get away with phony gestures of sympathy and friendship by posting their feelings instead of demonstrating the true behaviors of a friend.

OBSESSIVE TEXTERS!

You see it all the time. A husband and wife and their children are sitting down at a restaurant and instead of the husband and wife, let alone the children, engaging in conversation, they are texting other people on their phones. It is quite a remarkable site to behold. It defies all logic. Why are you more concerned about your "texting friends" than communicating with your own loved ones sitting right across from you at the table?

EMAIL IS OVERUSED.

Why can't people simply take a few minutes to personally discuss or call on the phone to resolve a problem? Today, everyone focuses more on documenting their efforts instead of working to resolve issues. I call it the "cover your ass" way of doing business. Everyone is so afraid to make a decision without documenting it in a 10 page email chain.

I especially love work colleagues that always use the "we sent out an email" about any new policy. They are usually referring to an email that probably went out more than a year ago. What if I just came on board the company eight months ago? How am I supposed to be held accountable for an email sent out a year before I arrived?

And to further insult everyone's intelligence and to make sure everyone covers their ass, we often find ourselves the recipients of the same email directive from three or four different people. The first email is from the person sending the directive. The second then comes from your boss within 30 minutes to reiterate the importance of the first email and to document that they followed up, so that a year down the road they can also say, "I reminded them of the directive." Then often, within a half hour of the second email, a third will arrive from a higher up level of management. And then the fourth is from the do-gooder at the boss's level that feels the need to make a comment. And then after all of that, we sometimes get lucky enough to receive a fifth email from the idiot who replies to "all" when he has a question for the original email sender!

Now in the modern world of business, we are expected to receive work emails on our cell phones. And people wonder why I say that the first thing I am going to do when I retire is throw the cell phone in the garbage.

Does Anyone Know How to Just Enjoy Silence?

I think many people have forgotten that we are human beings, and we benefit greatly from just simply relaxing. Everyone today seems to think we have to constantly be entertained or stimulated. Having instant communications at our hands has caused people to think human beings have the attributes of a computer, so they expect immediate responses when they call or text.

The excessive bombardment of information, emails, texts, and media updates are making life less fulfilling. Let's think about it. Technology was supposed to make our lives easier. Instead, it is making our lives more hectic. All this information is at our fingertips. It seems wonderful at first, until we realize it is ruling our lives.

Every business now wants us to register for their updates or participate in a survey every time we buy a product. So, we get stupid alerts from their stores every day. They forget that everyone is doing this, so it is often not unusual to receive many alerts from various stores throughout the day. It is exhausting. It creates unnecessary stress.

Let's turn off our phones and go for a walk along the river or lake. Why not try sitting on the front porch and spend an evening daydreaming or reminiscing?

WHEN DID EVERYONE GET SO BUSY?

Now it seems with the digital age, that everyone is too busy to even buy their own groceries. I wonder… how many people are no longer going to meet their future spouse now that they won't have the opportunity to bump into that beautiful lady with a grocery cart? Family members no longer call to invite us to Thanksgiving, but instead they text to invite. *Did I miss your getting elected President? You really are that busy that you can't personally call me once or twice a year to invite me to a dinner?*

Does anyone ever stop to think about how all this technology is changing the way we human beings meet and interact? People no longer come over to visit while sitting on the front porch. Young people today don't know what it is like to sit in the shade and crank away on an old-time ice cream freezer while talking with their grandfather. Nor do they appreciate the relaxing old-time 4th of July celebrations at home with family and playing a slow game of croquet on the front lawn. We put on our own fireworks show with sparklers and old fashioned firecrackers when I was a kid, surrounded by our relatives and family. We didn't have to go to some fireworks extravaganza surrounded by complete strangers, where it takes an hour to park, an hour to walk to the event, an hour to get back to the car, and then another hour in traffic in order to get home.

Just a generation ago, everyone visited and socialized with each other. Go to a family get-together today, and what do we see? Half the people in the room are busy texting some unseen persons on their mobile devices. Something has gone profoundly wrong when

a kid sits in a living room with parents and grandparents, but he spends the whole day talking to a small
device in his hand.

CHAPTER 2

Our Coddled Little Children

WHAT HAPPENED TO THE CHILDHOOD I GREW UP KNOWING?

I am convinced that generations born after 1985 have truly missed out on the fun and joy my generation experienced as kids. The fundamental difference is in how children today play and how I played. For example, kids today are not learning to play with their imagination. It seems that parents today feel the need to enroll their children in various activities instead of allowing them free time to play. It seems as soon as children become toddlers these days, they have a cell phone or some other gadget shoved into their hands to keep them quiet.

What fun we had! Some of the best play time I experienced as a child was spending an entire Saturday playing in the dirt. My dad allowed us a pretty large play area behind the barn in the backyard for us to play. We would disappear for the entire day, only going to the house to use the bathroom or eat lunch. My mom never wondered where we were during the day. She would, however, get worried if we failed to show up for supper.

Kids today aren't even allowed to be left alone for one minute to spend carefree time amusing themselves. Playing as a child is an important part of learning. In my play-dirt-construction-days, I reasoned out the fundamentals of such things as dam building. I was a realistic child, often creating massive reservoirs, only to have the dam fail and flood the village downstream. We built elaborate farms and towns with sticks and bricks. I would build a hay barn out of bricks and take the grass clippings that were piled in the corner of the yard, and make miniature hay bales to stack in the barn. My mom had the uncanny sense to always pop out the back door just as our make believe "hay barn" caught on fire.

Since we were from Oklahoma, there was always the devastating "tornado" to reduce our work to rubble after we tired of our latest creation, only to rebuild another, that would inevitably be destroyed by another "tornado," "flood," or "earthquake." My brother used to get so angry at me for destroying our farms that often took days and even weeks to build.

What fun we literally had with simple things like sticks and bricks. George Carlin, in his television performance, "It's Bad for Ya," summed it up perfectly when he said, "Do kids today even know what a stick is?"

I don't think any kid today would know what you mean when you say, "Let's play army."

We often used sticks for guns and yes, and oh how terrible, we actually had toy rifles and guns. And you know what? I don't ever recall being confused as to the difference between a real gun and a toy gun, that the over-protective parents of today fuss over. We knew the difference because our parents taught us the difference.

When we were at my grandfather's farm, we would play army in the old barn hay loft. We would throw dirt and straw dust all over each other during our "bombing raids." Without free play like this, we are creating a generation of wimpy kids, who are growing up to be wimpy adults. Have you seen how kids dress today just to ride a bike? The knights of England wore less body armor. We have to quit overprotecting kids! I once was acting reckless on my bicycle after my dad had warned me to stop. I ignored his sound advice and proceeded to slide face first into the asphalt of our neighborhood street. There was no sympathy, no rush to coddle.

My dad simply said, "I told you to quit acting like an idiot."

I learned and never made the same mistake again. I spent a month walking around with a huge scab on my face as a further reminder of my foolish behavior.

We have to let children play on their own and with whomever they choose. It is important for them to learn to deal with their peers and learn how to deal with conflict.

THE OVERPRAISING OF LITTLE CHILDREN!

Unfortunately, the younger generation have been raised by parents who have seriously overcompensated to boost their children's self esteem. As a result, this new generation of Americans have been brought up with a seriously delusional view of their own self-importance. The root of this delusion is in the self-esteem movement that first became very popular in the 1970s.

Here is an example. How many times have we been to an awards ceremony where someone is being honored for their achievements? It never fails. When reading the biography of the guest of honor, we will almost always see the following; "George and Mary are the parents of three "amazing children." Really, you have to be kidding! What makes their children amazing? Did they come up with a cure for cancer? Did they win the Nobel Peace prize at age six?

Now, don't get me wrong, I love children. I have seven nieces and nephews, and I love them dearly. But I would not describe any of them as being amazing, not any more than I am amazing. I don't ever recall, observing any child that has walked into any room at any point in my life, where I stopped and gazed upon them in awe and amazement. I know I am being somewhat ridiculous here in my point, but that is precisely the point. Words have meanings. Overuse of words of praise results in the loss of their meaning.

These kids begin their life with a dishonest and inaccurate view of themselves and their place in the world. This mindset has resulted in the "Me" generation which wouldn't know the truth if it stared them in the face. The lack of truth in one's very fundamental make-up is dangerous to self and to society. This fundamental flaw in the upbringing of our young generation is beginning to show itself in profound ways in everyday American life.

WHEN DID PARENTS START WORRYING ABOUT GETTING IT RIGHT?

I was recently watching a commercial on TV. The gist of the commercial was some dad catering to his every son's needs, making his son's lunch for him, cutting the crusts off the little boy's sandwich, leaving cute little messages in his lunch box, and the whole time stressing as to whether his son thought he got it right. In the commercial, the dad resembled a butler instead of the boy's father. I almost wanted to throw up watching the commercial. Now, don't get me wrong. My parents, I am sure, always did what they thought was right for me. The difference is they did what they thought was right for me, not what I thought was right! And I can tell you when my parents made decisions, they certainly weren't concerned about my opinion. When did parents develop this subservient attitude toward their own children?

I doubt my grandparents or my parents ever tossed and turned wondering what their kids thought of their performance. Parents today are so busy competing to be their children's best friend instead of their parents. It is demonstrated in the little things. When I was a kid, we would have a birthday celebration, usually a cake and ice cream. Bigger parties were reserved for more milestone birthdays. What do we have today? Many kids grow up thinking their birthdays are some sort of national holidays, with extravaganzas that always seems to have to outdo the prior year's birthday. For the good of your children, learn to say, "No."

Overindulgence, though it makes parents feel good, is harming children. It is a root cause of the "me" mentality that so often manifests itself in young people today. We are creating young people with no sense of proportion or reality.

I find it comical to watch some of these "career parents" who run around all weekend and all day, trying to get everything done for their children. And then they spend the week complaining about how tired they are and how they never have any time. I have an idea for them. Maybe little Susie could just play soccer, instead of both soccer and softball? Then maybe her parents will have some time to rest before going to work Monday morning to make the money to pay for Susie's soccer career.

We have to teach kids about what it's like to make decisions in life, which means sometimes actually making choices and setting priorities. We must stop fussing over children. We are creating little spoiled brats.

Imagine the following scenario. A family gets together, and the meal is ready, and the focus is getting the youngest kids' plates filled first. Meanwhile,

Grandma, who spent hours making the meal, is left to be last in line. And to add further insult, these same little kids, get choice seating at the table, while adults find a place standing at the kitchen counter. Wow! Have things been turned upside down? Is it just me, or do any of you see the absurdity of adults standing while the little kids eat at the most comfortable chairs at the table? Please, parents must reassert themselves in the proper role as the ones in charge. Loving children does not require making ourselves subservient to them.

People Who Don't Believe in Spanking

As a child, I received plenty of spankings, and it didn't do me any harm. I love to watch these young mothers using their time-out methodology. People, we cannot reason with a two-year-old about the hot stove top. A spanking is the only way we are going to get that point across unless we want to just wait for the child to burn a little hand.

I once knew a young mother who was adamant about not spanking her child. By the time she had the third one, I noticed one day that she spanked one of her children. I remembered with a smile how just a few years before she had told me all about the time-out methodology that she felt would work better.

Some of the punishments I saw as a child would probably get a parent into trouble today. My grandfather would make a child kneel on a broomstick for a period of time. My dad would first make me squat in the corner for a period of time as the first line of discipline. Then if I moved before he said time was up, I might end up getting the belt. We also were the recipients of a few thumps on the ear or back of the head for misbehaving. That was a real effective one, as it not only had the element of pain, but of embarrassment, too.

My brothers and I thought it would be funny to hide the black belt that always was handily kept on top of the refrigerator. We got walloped for that prank. There were the times when we knew we had done something bad to really warrant a good whipping. We would plead mercifully with our eyes hoping our mother would step in on our behalf to intervene when Dad was coming with that belt. Most likely though, they acted like a team and surrounded us at the kitchen table.

It always seemed that among us three boys at least one or two of us averaged getting the belt once a week for doing something mean to our younger sister. We learned that our grandparents were more bark than bite though. One time, my brothers and I were staying overnight with our grandmother, and we had aggravated her to her wits' end about something. She spent about 20 minutes chasing us around the bed and then only managed to give a slight tap with the fly swatter. We knew our grandmother had a soft heart for us grandchildren.

Even through all those spankings though, as I look back, I don't recall ever feeling unjustly treated. I believe this is because deep down, even as a kid, I knew when I had done something really wrong.

I also learned that there were consequences to certain behaviors, and my parents were not the kind to just let me get away with bad behavior. I once talked back to my dad while sitting on my bike. Being a dumb child, I thought I could outrun my dad on my bike. What a surprise I got when the bike suddenly stopped dead in its tracks in the street! Kids never think their dad can run that fast. As kids, too, we never seemed to be smart enough to realize that even if we ran away, we eventually had to come back home and receive the punishment in the end.

SCHOOLS ARE RUINING YOUNG MINDS.

I remember recently a teenager in the same room where we were discussing the year of my dad's birth, which was 1942. During the discussion, we mentioned that was when the United States was engaged in World War II. The school propaganda was evident when this teenager commented that was the year we locked up all those Japanese people. Now, of course, that is a part of World War II history, but really, that is the most important thing that our schools focus on when discussing the history of World War II? Do they learn about the millions of people that the Japanese murdered in China? Do they discuss the naked aggression that the Japanese perpetuated on the mostly peace-seeking world? Do these young students even know that 70 to 85 million people were killed worldwide due to the aggression of the three countries of Japan, Germany and Italy? Instead, our schools focus on the 120,000 Japanese interned in camps, humanely by the way. The 70 to 85 million people killed worldwide likely resulted in another 100 million or more other people whose lives were affected by being orphaned or widowed, but we are going to focus on the 120,000 people who, though inconvenienced, did live and get back to a normal life after the war.

I watched a program on TV in which a professor discussed how an extremely large percentage of high school seniors couldn't even pass the Basic Citizenship test that immigrants are required to complete. This professor said exactly what I have already observed for years. Since the standards have been "dummied down" from the grade schools all the way through high school, then the next places to "dummy down" are the universities.

No wonder that a member of Congress, with a degree in economics from a major university, can genuinely believe in a plan such as the Green New Deal. How else could someone with a degree in economics actually believe in such an unrealistic plan? In these college graduates' minds, they actually believe in the unattainable.

And now the failure of our public schools is on full display as we see a large percentage of young people who believe that socialism is a viable option. How many times does socialism have to fail for people to see the failure that it is? Do these schools even discuss the former Soviet Union, North Korea, Vietnam, Cuba, and Venezuela? What better real-life lesson can we get than current day Venezuela? Yet, we still have these idiots professing that it can work. I guess I shouldn't be surprised.

I once mentioned Mikhail Gorbachev in a conversation with a person born around 1984, and he asked me, "Who is Gorbachev?" A central figure during the fall of the Berlin Wall that occurred during this person's childhood, and he doesn't know the name? That is a monumental failure of our education system.

MANY TEACHERS ARE NOT GIVEN THE RESPECT THEY DESERVE!

I don't blame some teachers today for having a bad attitude. The teachers are either attacked for trying to implement discipline, or the truly good teachers who are trying to educate young people with the truth are beaten down by the politically correct directives forced upon them by the school administration. The news is always full of stories about parents criticizing a teacher for this or that. They even attack teachers who dare to discipline the parent's "darling little angels" when they do something wrong.

When I was a kid, I knew damn good and well, if I did something wrong at school, my parents were going to be on the teacher's side, not mine. And parents had each other's backs when dealing with each other's children. I learned from an early age that my parents expected me to reflect in a positive way because my behavior was a reflection of them. I remember vividly an experience I learned from my mom. At the end of one school year, I learned that a classmate was being held back, and I made fun of her. Let me tell you, as soon as I got home from school that very day, my mom already knew what I had done. My classmate's mother had called my mother to tell her what happened. My mother didn't criticize the other mother; she did the right thing and corrected my bad behavior and quickly.

People today do not seem to demonstrate a sense of community. Today when a parent or teacher dares to criticize a rude student's behavior, the parents of the bad kid seem to gang up on the teacher or other parent, wrongly defending their child no matter what. These parents never seem to be around demanding that their students receive the best education. They seem to only be around to accuse the school of mistreating their child.

WHAT IS WITH ALL THESE KIDS LABELED WITH ATTENTION DEFICIT DISORDER?

You know what we called these kids that demonstrated such behavior when I was a kid? Undisciplined! Now, don't get me wrong. There are some legitimately troubled kids, but when I was a kid, they would have been assigned to special education. We can look hard at some of these kids' behaviors. Much of it stems completely from the lack of discipline by their parents, beginning at an early age. Some of these kids would benefit greatly from a good old-fashioned spanking, not from medicating.

I AM TIRED OF THE "IT'S FOR THE CHILDREN" COMMENT.

Sorry, folks, but the world does not revolve around children.

AND NOW WE NEED TO TALK ABOUT THE MILLENNIALS.

First of all, your generation is not as significant and special as you think. I can name a hundred people from other generations who have produced more for humanity than you can ever imagine in your little self-absorbed world.

From what I have seen of the millennial generation, they are self-absorbed, narcissistic, coddled, spoiled, entitled, childish, shallow, uneducated, self-important, and weak in mind and body. A hundred years from now, nothing of great significance will come to mind from them, when the history books speak of the millennial generation other than that they had fast texting skills.

So, they continue living in a self-absorbed world and texting friends with endless drivel about their mundane lives and how rough they have it. And please spare me in your job interview of how much you think your salary should be before you have even proven how skilled or productive you are. Many millennials feel entitled to a large salary right out of college and even openly make envious statements regarding those who receive a larger salary. What they haven't learned is that the person they are despising spent 20 plus years working to earn that large salary through the development of their skills and experience. From what I have seen, they seem to think they already know everything. It is nearly impossible to mentor or educate a millennial.

The millennial generation is a shallow group of people who show no respect or appreciation for anything that was sacrificed on their behalf, well before they were ever born. They sit and talk in their Internet cafes about the virtues of equality and freedom, and yet they show their ignorance about how they came to even have those gifts at their fingertips.

Now, don't get me wrong. There are a few good ones in the millennial generation. I would estimate about 5 percent who seem to get it when it comes to acting responsibly, like the adults they should be. It is so rare to find these gems, that I get excited and amazed when I get the chance to hire one of the exceptional members of their generation.

Now to be fair, one can hardly blame the millennials themselves. The millennials are the way they are because they were coddled and raised up on pedestals by their parents. They are the children and grandchildren of the baby boomers, who are at times quite the selfish generation themselves. The baby boomers have saddled my generation and the millennial generation with an outrageous national debt to pay for their benefits that they demanded of their elected officials.

These baby boomers were spoiled by the Greatest Generation, who were born between the 1900s and 1920s because their parents did not want them to ever want and suffer the way they did. Unfortunately, the baby boomers, in many cases did not share the stories of their parents, the Greatest Generation, with their children. For those who don't know what I mean by the Greatest Generation, let me define it. The Greatest Generation were the millions of Americans who lived, sacrificed, suffered, died, or survived during the Great Depression and World War II.

The trivialities that Americans complain about today are embarrassing when compared to the real struggles of the Greatest Generation. Most millennials today have never heard of things such as soup lines and rationing books. They have probably never heard of or have been taught how many American lives were lost to take the island of Iwo Jima during World War II. They could never imagine soldiers having to postpone a wedding because they couldn't get a furlough during wartime. They couldn't imagine an out-of-work person offering to work just for a meal during the Great Depression, instead of demanding a free meal.

The millennials, as evidenced by their rudimentary grasp of spelling and punctuation, certainly have never experienced the joy of spelling out words while under pressure in front of a classroom on the chalkboard. No wonder they cannot handle scrutiny in the workforce. Do schools even have chalkboards anymore? Or have they been deemed too dangerous to the environment because children might inhale secondhand chalk dust?

We are in big trouble when this generation gets the chance to run our country. Thankfully, I will be dead by then!

Many millennials, I am sure, will be offended by the many "trigger" words in this chapter, and I hope they can find a "safe space" to recover.

32

CHAPTER 3

The Exaggeration of Everything

Watching the news each day, I often find myself wondering if I am completely surrounded by idiots and fanatics, who seem to blow everything out of proportion. The amount of time given to the trivialities of life is beginning to wear thin.

EVERYTHING IS A CATASTROPHE!

I remember when I was a kid; there was one local 30-minute TV news show and one 30-minute national TV program available. Now, we are bombarded with an endless array of so-called "news" stories. Everything is exaggerated and labeled as a "crisis," "life-threatening," "unusual," or "record-breaking." And I am sick to death of the so-called "weather experts" connecting any unusually high rainfall or other event to "climate change." Of course, we have climate change. It's known as the start of a new day. Sorry, Mr. Weatherman, but when there is a weather front moving through the East Coast with a chance of tornadoes, there are not 20 to 50 million people at risk for a tornado. Apparently these so-called weather reporters have never observed a tornado and realized that a tornado is typically only about a quarter of a mile to a mile wide and usually is on the ground for about 30 minutes to an hour. I would say hardly big enough to affect 50 million people!

How am I such an expert on tornadoes, you may ask? I am not an expert, but I grew up and lived in Oklahoma and have enough common sense from observing the weather to understand tornadoes. I also have enough common sense to not go out in the thunderstorm or go out into the blizzard without the guys on the weather channel warning me it would be dangerous. How many people do they think brave a blizzard just for the fun of it, or don't know to put on a coat when the temperature is 5° F outside? News reporters are so egotistical that they apparently think the average American is an idiot and couldn't survive without their advice.

Recently the media has resorted to exaggerating hailstorms to make a connection to "climate change." For example, on June 30, there was a heavy hailstorm in Guadalajara, Mexico. The headlines all read: "Hailstorm Dumps Several Feet of Hail" or something to that effect. Some media were slightly less misleading by reporting "several feet accumulated." I have witnessed some heavy hailstorms, and they only usually last 10 to 15 minutes. They never last long enough to dump more than a few inches of hail at a time, but the Mexico hail report showed pictures of several feet of hail in the streets. And that was the give away to what really transpired. Yes, the hail had collected by being washed into constricted ditches and streets where it piled up to several feet. But interestingly, the nearby buildings with flat roofs only showed a few inches of hail on top. This is devious and evil. This is how propaganda gets started.

Do these weather reporters realize how stupid they look standing on the side of the road during a snowstorm to show us ice in a skillet? And don't even get me started on the "wimpification" of our kids today when it comes to the weather and school closures. I remember anxiously watching the morning news as a child praying that our school would be closed due to the snow. It rarely happened unless there was a blizzard. Now school is closed if there are a couple inches of snow on the ground. The schools have now started closing because the wind chill gets below a certain level. Last time I checked, most schools have heating inside, and they don't conduct class outside during a snowstorm. I don't recall ever hearing of a classmate freezing to death on the way to school, as our school bus had heat, and my mom didn't make us stand out in the cold until the bus was within a few stops of the house.

The incessant complaining public get so upset that the roads aren't cleared right away after major snowstorms. These people apparently think their city has a snowplow for every city block. It never occurs to these complainers to get off their butts and pick up a shovel and help clear the street in front of their own homes. Even worse are the entitled people of the world who have the audacity to sue business owners because they fall on ice in the parking lot. They even sue because they slip on the sand the property owner puts down to cover ice and make it safer for the public. These are the same people who expect federal assistance to help clean up broken tree branches from their yards after ice storms. Their problems are always someone else's fault, never the result of their own stupidity. In addition, we are supposed to feel sorry for the same type of people when they can't afford to rebuild their houses destroyed by fire. Typically, they can't "afford" home insurance, even though they stand there on camera smoking cigarettes that cost more in a year than what a homeowner policy would cost during the same period.

What is it with people who empty the grocery store shelves of everything because we might have an ice storm for a couple of days? Those who live in any major US city are not going to starve to death. Many live within walking distance of a grocery store, or the next-door neighbor is just 20 steps away. Don't worry. The food delivery trucks will restock the city's grocery stores. And why, during a snowstorm, do the shelves seem to empty of bottled water? For Pete's sake, if we run out of water, we can always eat the snow!

What is with this need to provide 24-hour live coverage of every hurricane that comes ashore? What can possibly change from minute to minute that requires this extent of coverage? I am quite aware that a hurricane's winds are likely to exceed over 200 miles per hour, so I don't need some stupid reporter wading through water and leaning into the wind to get the picture to prove it. One day, I am convinced… we are going to witness one of these reporters being decapitated live on TV by a flying street sign.

I am also getting tired of every snowstorm or hurricane being called "unusual," "historic," or "unprecedented." Have any of these people who say such things ever read about the great blizzard of 1887 or the New England Hurricane of 1938? In 1900, there were an estimated 8,000 people killed in the category 4 Galveston Hurricane. The media goes on and on about 10 to 20 people who die in a hurricane which is quite a remarkable improvement compared to other hurricanes in weather history. Sorry to sound callous… but with multiple, advance warnings and satellite technology, there is really no reason for anyone to die in storms anymore. If someone does die during a hurricane, it's likely because he or she ignored the many warnings to evacuate.

I especially love when the weather man or woman on national TV feels the need to advise people on what to do during a tornado. The news people who report from New York City have never even experienced an Oklahoma or Texas tornado, but yet they feel they are more informed than the general public that have grown up with these storms their entire lives. I recently saw a female weather lady advising the people of Arkansas to make sure that they wear shoes to the storm shelter because there might be nails and other hazards around when they leave the storm shelter. Does she think all people in Arkansas live like hillbillies and walk around in overalls and bare feet? Did she develop her impressions of people from Arkansas from the old Bugs Bunny cartoon called "Hillbilly Hare?"

I also get so tired of the trite descriptions of natural disasters. It is the same anytime a tornado destroys a town. The media or some witness says, "It looks like a bomb went off or it looks like a war zone." No, it looks like a tornado just destroyed the town.

The media are just as noncreative when describing an earthquake. They always say the same thing. "An earthquake rocked the country today." They apparently never heard of the words shook or rattled. And a major blizzard is not a "bomb cyclone." It is simply a blizzard. It is nothing new. Blizzards have occurred often, and until recently, they were never referred to as a "bomb cyclone." And of course, we no longer have just a simple hurricane. They are now "superstorms."

Winter weather used to be simply described as a series of incoming cold fronts, and not named like we name hurricanes. I cringe when I hear deep snow described as "snowmageddon." Oh and don't forget all the warnings about how dangerous the Texas heat is in August! Most of us do not work on farms or anywhere outdoors such as in construction, so I think most people will survive as they transfer themselves from air-conditioned offices to air-conditioned cars and then back to air-conditioned homes. I think we will survive standing outside in the heat for five minutes as we fuel up our SUVs with immediate air conditioning and the holder for our ice-cold water bottle waiting inside.

It is getting so ridiculous, that a mere drop of rain or a clap of thunder initiates around the clock reporting on live TV. It becomes major around-the-clock news just to talk about rain. We now have sirens blown to warn of severe thunderstorms, which I predict is going to cause people to eventually ignore the sirens. They should only be used for actual tornadoes. News reporters now even interrupt television shows and movies during minor thunderstorms just to tell us that there is nothing to worry about!

WHAT IS IT WITH THE PEOPLE WHO REFUSE TO BUDGE AND SEEK SAFETY FROM AN IMMINENT HURRICANE OR VOLCANO ERUPTION?

There is always the "tough guy" who says something like, "This is my home, and by God, I am not going to budge no matter what." Ask Harry Truman, not the president, but that guy by the same name who said such a thing back before Mount Saint Helen's was going to erupt… oh, wait a minute! No one can ask him. He is buried under hundreds of feet of ash and debris. He sure showed that volcano who was the boss! We always see a similar person after every hurricane who eventually gets to tell his story on the

Discovery channel about how he almost drowned when the storm surge swept his house away.

I am really getting tired of the word "apocalyptic" getting thrown around. Recently, a large part of England had a major power outage. In an interview, someone had the audacity to describe it as "apocalyptic!" We now have people freaking out if the power goes out for four hours? I am surprised the power outage wasn't also immediately linked to global climate change. What are these lunatics that freak out over a power outage going to do when an asteroid hits Earth? Now, that may qualify as apocalyptic.

CHAPTER 4

What Happened to Patriotism?

The changes in our society are most profoundly demonstrated in the behaviors and trends among the younger population. The new generation of people coming of age, those of the generation born after 1985, have unfortunately been raised without the same values that prior generations would have instilled in them from birth. Do the schools even teach a class called "Civics" today? Patriotic people are often painted as racists or "white supremacists." People who demonstrate patriotism are now viewed as controversial?

WHEN DID PEOPLE BECOME TOO LAZY TO STAND AND SHUT-UP FOR ONE MINUTE DURING "THE STAR SPANGLED BANNER?"

I think this demonstrates another issue. Kids today, since they are brainwashed with politically correct revisions of history, show no appreciation or sense of pride when the flag is brought out onto a field before a ball game. I don't understand why others do not get chills up their spines or even sometimes become teary-eyed when "The Star Spangled Banner" is sung and played.

Let me educate some people about the etiquette regarding the flag. It is very simple. When we are at a sporting event or other public function involving "The Star Spangled Banner," we do the following:

1. Stand up.
2. Shut up.
3. Take our hats off.
4. Hold our hand over our hearts.
5. Focus entirely on the flag.
6. Sing along if so inclined, and if we actually know the words.
7. Clap at the end to show our appreciation and respect for our country.

I doubt that schools teach the story of "The Star Spangled Banner" anymore. It is so important to know that the flag represents the sacrifices that were made and the lives that were spent to secure our freedom.

And let me tell you professional sports players: no one wants to listen to your political statements about how you are treated badly in this country while you take home your multimillion-dollar salaries. The fans that have saved up to what amounts to a small life savings to take their families to just one of your games… certainly are not interested in your "sob story."

These people who cannot respect our very own National Anthem demonstrate how selfish and narcissistic they are. The National Anthem is something that should make us think beyond ourselves and our egos.

OVERUSE OF THE LOWERING OF THE FLAG

This sacred tradition has become so common now that it is losing its meaning. Let's go back to lowering the flag for truly significant national events. It seems that the flag is now being lowered for some reason or another every other week.

PATRIOTS WHO FLY THE UNITED STATES FLAG ON THEIR VEHICLES

Although you may have good intentions, please don't disrespect our flag by flying it as if it were some trivial accessory for your vehicle.

CHAPTER 5

Basic Manners

I believe basic manners have been on the decline for the last generation. When society continually tells its children, all that matters is their own happiness; then, decorum and consideration for others is going to be a casualty.

WHEN DID COMMON COURTESY AND HYGIENE GO OUT THE DOOR?

How many times do we go to the grocery store and have to go through two or three different carts before we find one that is clean enough to place our food we want to purchase? Who are these people who are so disgusting, egotistical, arrogant, and obviously disturbed that they think I should feel privileged to have them leave me their snot-soaked tissue in the grocery cart? I used to park cars as a valet, and I actually encountered people frequently who would get out of their car when parking and actually try to hand me a used tissue to throw away for them.

These people are only one step below the inconsiderate smokers who think it is acceptable to throw their cigarette butts out the door and onto the sidewalk. No, I take that back. They may only be one step below the people who throw their used chewing gum on the sidewalk right in front of the door of the same grocery store. No, I take that back. They are similar to the jerks that spit their snot out onto the sidewalk in front of the grocery store for everyone else to step in.

Let's discuss dog owners. I find it interesting that dog owners always take their dogs on walks down the street, so their dogs can pee or poop in someone else's front yard, but never in their own yard. I am so tired of this excessive love of dogs anyway. Not everyone thinks your dog is so precious. And I certainly don't agree with those dog owners who say that a dog's mouth is cleaner than a human's, right after they kiss their dog on the mouth and let the dog slobber all over their faces. They usually say this not long after that same dog has drunk out of the toilet bowl and then proceeded to lick its own butt. Technically a dog's mouth may be cleaner than a human's, but that doesn't mean that its mouth is sanitary or clean!

Why are dog owners so proud of their dogs anyway? I mean I can see being proud of kids, but a dog? The owners didn't conceive it or give birth to it. They don't share DNA. Why do dog owners feel they need to let their dog make contact with me while walking down the sidewalk? Trust me. I don't feel the need to greet and get acquainted with people's dogs. Why do dog owners feel the need to pressure me into obligatory praise of their smelly dogs?

I especially love the dog owners who say, "He is just being friendly," right after their dog snarls, growls and barks at me while jumping on me on the sidewalk. Why bother with the leash if it is a 20-foot leash and still allows the dog to jump all over me with its muddy paws and to scratch me with its nails? After these encounters, the dog owners will often give a begrudging, "I'm sorry," as they walk off. Imagine if I as a complete stranger were to run up to them screaming and hollering and put my hands all over them because I was just friendly. It would be about as pleasant as being surprised by snarling dogs lunging at me from out of nowhere.

What is it with the people who have so little concern for others that they don't even have the courtesy to wash their hands after using the restroom? My fellow males, this goes for going number 1 and not just number 2. I find it creepy that a great many people don't even wash their hands after number 2. If not for everyone else's sake, at least for their own… everyone should do it! How can people go around with their own poop on their hands all day?

I also personally dislike it when people take reading materials into the bathroom to read while pooping. It is pretty gross when you think about it. I don't want to touch that book or newspaper after it is held with the hand that wiped a butt in the bathroom. Some of you may be reading this book in the bathroom, right? People, please don't answer the phone while in the bathroom. Show some class and spare others from having to listen to such bodily functions while talking on the phone.

How many times do we find ourselves standing in line patiently at the store counter, only to have someone just walk up and interrupt the transaction in progress, because they just have a "question?" I once confronted such a person, who responded as if I were the one being rude.

What about the people who go to movies and insist on talking out loud right up until the actual movie dialogue begins? These morons are so stupid, they don't realize that many clues to a storyline are often found right at the beginning of the film even when only credits and music are playing. These are the same people who we hear later, asking, and further ruining the other movie patrons' experience, "Now, why did he do that?"

These people are also the same ones that manage to kick the back of our seats repeatedly during the movie and don't realize how offensive it is for them to prop their dirty shoes or even their bare feet up on the chair next to other people. It is so commonplace for these frustrations to occur, that I rarely go to a movie theater anymore. I almost forgot… when do we find ourselves fortunate enough to have an almost empty movie theater, and when we do, people find a reason to sit right next to or behind us when there are hundreds of other seats open?

Let's talk about people at buffet restaurants or any other type of restaurant for that matter. When we take our kids to a restaurant, it is not acceptable to let our kids throw food on the floor because someone else will clean it up later! For the people who are filling their plates at the buffet, they should please wait to eat the food piled on their plates… until leaving the serving area. We must also realize how gross it is for us to lick our fingers after stuffing our faces at the buffet line. I have to touch that spoon that is used by those people, too, and I really don't find it appetizing to have their saliva all over it. Just because it is a buffet, this doesn't mean we have to act like pigs. For Heaven's sake, we can go back for as many visits as we like. We don't have to pile two feet of food on that little plate each visit! A friend of mine once told me he saw a rather heavyset woman at a buffet line, with a loaded plate in each hand, and an egg roll in her mouth. I can't explain it any better than that.

The passive aggressive, self-appointed traffic control officers, who drive below the speed limit in the fast lane… why? They know who they are, and they know good and well that they are annoying people with their self-righteous behavior. They never know, that the person trying to get around… may really have a life-threatening emergency.

PEOPLE WHO LICK THEIR FINGERS WHEN EATING, COUNTING MONEY, OR BAGGING OUR GROCERIES!

First, unless we are starving to death, there is absolutely no reason to lick food off our fingers when dining out with other people. Napkins take care of that. Some people are not just content to lick the tips of their fingers. I have seen people at restaurants insert entire fingers in their mouths to consume every drop of food available.

For people who lick their fingers when counting out money… do they ever stop to think about where that money has been? Let me give everyone a visual. Think of who, what and where that dollar bill has been… places such as a strip club? How many people keep their money in their underwear or sock? How many of those dollar bills have fallen on public bathroom floors or have been fished out of toilet bowls? I once saw a lady pull out a sweaty $20 bill from her bra to pay a cashier once.

The worst offenders in the finger-licking category must be the people who bag our groceries at the store and lick their fingers to get a grip on the plastic bag. Then after licking their fingers, they proceed to touch my produce and other food products, spreading their saliva all over everything. They might as well spit in my food! The worst offenders seem to be middle-aged to older females. These are the same females that have the disgusting habit of using their spit to wet their kids' hair down in a pinch. Yuck!

PEOPLE WHO CUT IN LINE AT THE GROCERY STORE

How many times have we seen this? Three or more people are waiting in line at a congested checkout register. A cashier opens the adjacent register and says, "I can help the next person in line." Nine times out of ten, the last person in the line at the congested register will jump over to the newly opened line. I am not sure when "next in line" means "last in line."

PEOPLE WHO BLOCK THE SHOPPING AISLE AT THE STORE

What is wrong with these people who insist on dominating the entire aisle at the store while they decide on which soap to buy? How complicated is buying soap and shampoo anyway? I see people all the time spending half an hour in the soap and shampoo aisle sniffing the shampoo and deodorant like it is the first time they have ever seen either. It reminds me of some National Geographic footage of gorillas when the primates spot a strange object in the grass in the jungle.

PEOPLE WHO THROW USED DIAPERS OUT IN THE PARKING LOT!

People who throw used diapers in parking lots are obviously disturbed people. Their behavior is no different than them personally taking a crap on the same pavement. How would anyone like it if someone squatted and took a dump beside their car in the parking lot? And then, how would anyone like it if they proceeded to accidently step into that pile of crap? Well, let me tell everyone. Stepping onto a used diaper in the parking lot is no less unpleasant.

PEOPLE WHO ARE TOO LAZY TO PUT THE SHOPPING CART INTO THE HOLDING CAGE!

How lazy do you have to be that you don't have enough consideration for other people's property that you can't walk that extra 20 feet to put the grocery cart away properly? These people will almost certainly be the first to complain when a cart rolls into their vehicle.

PEOPLE WHO LITTER!

People who engage in this behavior, I believe, have to be some of the shallowest people in the world. It was sickening to visit the Grand Canyon of all places and see large numbers of empty water bottles littering the side of the canyon. How anyone cannot be humbled and show enough respect for such an amazing place astounds me!

LANDSCAPERS AND HOMEOWNERS WHO USE BLOWERS TO DUMP THEIR DEBRIS ON EVERYONE ELSE!

I have never understood the logic of people who mow a lawn and then when done, think it is acceptable to blow the grass clippings and leaves from their yard into the public street. I have confronted such people and have often heard the following: "The wind is going to blow it into the street anyway."

"The wind blowing it into the street anyway" is not the same thing as someone blowing it into the street on purpose. People might as well just dump the debris directly into my yard because guess what happens? As soon as anyone blows debris into the street, it then is certainly very likely to end up in my yard, and then, I have to pick up the debris someone should have picked up and disposed of properly in the first place from their own yard!

PEOPLE WHO TREAT CELL PHONE LISTS AS THEIR OWN PRIVATE RADIO NETWORK

We have all experienced it. We are nice enough to give someone our cell phone number. Then we get these texts that are sent out in mass to many people including us. It is obvious some idiot managed to get our number and now treats it like we are part of some radio network. Some of these people who send out texts have no concept of boundaries or even basic manners. They send their mass communications out at all hours of the day. The other day, some self-righteous person who somehow has my cell number on a list, felt the need to send out a quote from the Bible to everyone at 6:50 a.m. I have my own Bible and certainly do not need someone sending me quotes out of it before I am barely out of bed.

So, to all nincompoops who hold people's cell phone data in your possession: you should remember that these are our cell phones… our property… you are using as your megaphone to make sure everyone knows how important and brilliant you are. That is disrespectful and rude. Texting should not be confused with social media posts. Each of us pays for our cell phones and service, not you. Some of us do not even have unlimited texting plans! Many of us even use our cell phones for work which should not be interrupted with your unimportant drivel, and we don't appreciate getting random doses of self-indulgent behavior broadcast at all hours.

PEOPLE WHO INSIST ON MAKING ME LISTEN TO THEIR LOUD MUSIC!

Everyone has a right to listen to any music they want, but why force others to listen to it? When we can hear the bass in someone's so-called rap music over our own television sets, someone has really overstepped the line of common courtesy. These are probably the same people that install loud mufflers on their vehicles so that everyone in the neighborhood is informed of their arrival home from the bar at 3 a.m.

These same people also think it is pleasant to listen to some guy whistling a tune as he goes down the sidewalk. Trust me, the whistling is not pretty; it is actually quite annoying.

CHAPTER 6

Gone are the Golden Days of Hollywood

WHY DOES SO-CALLED FAMILY TV HAVE TO BE SO CRASS?

Now, don't get me wrong. I am no prude by any means. I think crass humor can have its moments, but in small doses, and certainly not during so-called family programming on a Sunday night.

Call me old-fashioned, but some of the best comedy of all time were shows such as "The Carol Burnett Show" and "The Dean Martin Show." People like Jonathan Winters would have you in stitches from laughter without ever using one profane word.

Why is it that Hollywood never learns that the best high-grossing films are the clean ones that families and children can watch? It is getting pretty bad, when even now that I am an adult I get embarrassed watching TV with my parents because of some of the crude things the actors say and do. These shows are so crude and boring that they have become predictable. Do producers have to constantly resort to crude sexualized jokes about elderly people to get a laugh? Once or twice is funny, but when overdone your show has become predictable and actually quite boring.

I remember as a kid when the movies "Jaws" and "Airplane" were released. My parents were concerned that "Jaws" was too gory and "Airplane" was too dirty. By today's standards, those two movies are quite tame when compared to some of the graphic topics discussed on many so-called family television shows. I find it quite ironic that many of today's television shows are just as graphic as some R rated movie at times, but yet they are allowed to broadcast out over the entire network for all ages to see.

WHY DOES HOLLYWOOD RESORT TO CHEAP PRODUCTIONS THAT APPEAL TO THE LOWEST COMMON DENOMINATOR?

I remember the Hollywood of my childhood. We waited with great anticipation for the next movie. Hollywood used to be creative and actually produced magical movies that truly transported you to other worlds and often inspired people to aspire to higher things.

There are fewer and fewer of what I call the iconic actors who are truly professional and always appear in quality productions. Of all the modern actors today, I can honestly think of one true actor that represents dignity and that is Robert Duvall. I miss John Wayne, Lauren Bacall, Barbara Stanwyck, Maureen O'Hara, and James Stewart. Talk about the "Heyday of Hollywood."

Some of the most glamorous and beautiful Hollywood women from previous generations never had to wear a dress to the Academy Awards that showed their crack or their navel, to prove that they were sexy, classy, and beautiful.

Now, what do we get, one mundane so-called "reality show" after the other. Just when I think they can't think of anything more boring to watch, they pump out something even more awful. Something is terribly wrong when we can have 80 channels available on a Sunday night and literally, and I really mean literally, I can't find one show that even seems worth watching.

Hollywood used to exercise a sense of artistic integrity when producers felt it beneath them to produce such garbage, even if they thought people might pay for it and watch it. Not anymore! Now, we are bombarded with shows about allegedly everyday people. These shows are just reworked versions of the same theme of debauchery and stupidity. These shows certainly do not relate to my experiences growing up. They are always the same stupid show where we put a bunch of self-important people together and they then create invented drama. Then these so-called "reality television families" become celebrities!

MOVIES THAT PORTRAY WOMEN AS THE RATIONAL HERO, BUT MEN AS AGGRESSIVE AND THOUGHTLESS

Has anyone noticed the new trend in movies to always make sure we have the politically correct version of the modern-day heroine? Pick almost any modern-day action movie or science fiction movie. There will typically be three main characters, with one being a woman. They always portray the woman with superior intelligence to the men. They portray the men as self-destructive creatures who can't control their aggression without the female heroine restraining them.

NATURE SHOWS HAVE BECOME POLITICAL.

Ever listen to documentaries about nearly any major endangered animal, and you will always hear the following or a derivation thereof: "The great white shark is naturally non-aggressive and has no real predator, except man."

I don't know about you, but when I encounter a great white shark, I really don't care if he has a motive or is simply acting out of instinct when its hundreds of razor-sharp teeth make me into mincemeat. If we really listen to any naturalists or environmentalists, we would think the only solution for the world is for us human beings to simply go out and kill ourselves to rid the planet of our evil presence. These same scientists who proclaim the theory of evolution ignore a basic scientific truth… that man has evolved to the top of the food chain. For some reason, if a bear is viewed at the top of a food chain, that is viewed as acceptable, but for humans, it must not be so.

I am quite frankly glad we have become the top of the food chain. I don't know about everyone else, but I feel much better that we evolved to have the intelligence to invent weapons that can kill a bear when it attacks. I guess these scientists would rather go back 11,000 years ago and be preyed upon by animals such as the short-faced bear. Look it up. When I learned about the short-faced bear, it sure made me glad I was born when I was born and to not have to be worried about being eaten by one at any given moment.

I could not think of anything worse than a grizzly bear, except for a grizzly bear that also rose to the top of the food chain and has a gun in addition to his teeth and claws!

CHAPTER 7

The Self-Anointed Media

The so-called unbiased and self-anointed media really makes my skin crawl. They spew false and misleading information, and often tell outright lies to the American people. They then have the audacity to act offended when people dare criticize their "sacrosanct" institution.

Today's media elite show nothing but clear disdain for anyone who dares live outside of California or New York. I wonder how many of these so-called informed media elite, who claim to know what the pulse of America is, have ever been inside the states of Oklahoma or Kansas. These elitists live in a cocoon of their big cities and have no idea what "mainstream" America is like. These same elitists live their lives thinking the single best places in the world are New York City, Los Angeles and Paris. They claim to be informed and enlightened but wouldn't condescend to visit a city such as Omaha, Nebraska or Fargo, North Dakota.

The talk shows on the cable networks only interview fellow elitists who live in the same isolation of New York, Washington DC, and Los Angeles. It would be interesting if they would spend more time interviewing people from the rest of America for a change. I think they may very well find that the rest of America couldn't care less about what the media elites believe and say are the most important matters facing our nation.

We now have wacko conspiracy theories animated regularly by the so-called major news. Literally crazy people, who the media would never have allowed on the air 20 years ago, are now given equal time to spew their ideas as if they were legitimate. All of the news commentary shows operate under the same formula, giving equal time to both sides… even when one side is obviously absurd.

THERE IS NO LONGER A NEUTRAL MEDIA IN AMERICA.

Think about it. The so-called conservative media outlets have really become a branch of the Republican Party. Likewise, the liberal media outlets are a branch of the Democratic Party. Just look at the headlines on most news outlets. They are often subjective statements, disguised as questions. Has anyone really looked at cable news lately? The majority of the time is spent editorializing. There really is no "proper news desk."

And now every other story is "breaking news." Give me a break. A bus going over a cliff in China is not breaking news in America. It may very well be in Beijing, but not in my hometown in Texas.

Let's be honest. The media outlets are really more like political action committees with their own agendas. The media are constantly trying to shape public opinion. They are getting so emboldened that they hardly even bother to disguise their bias anymore.

The media also uses the "trickery of words and phrases" to distort the facts. They get away with it by technically saying they report exactly what people said or did. However, they distort through editing and eliminating the context of speeches and statements made by their enemies. For example, the media has an agenda to convince the American people that the Russians hacked the 2016 presidential election. Now, there is probably proof that the Russians hacked into the Democratic Party's emails, but that is not the same as hacking the election.

By continually stating over and over on television that the Russians hacked the election, the media are subconsciously planting the belief in the uneducated viewers' minds that the Russians did in fact hack our election process. Let's be clear. To have truly hacked our election, the Russians would have had to hack the ballot counting databases across the country and actually have manipulated the tallies to in fact "hack the election." But this did not happen. Notice how the media are experts at using language and words to distort facts and opinions?

I also get tired of the media giving so much attention to groups of protesters. Through editing and camera angles, they make a crowd of 100 look like a 1,000. And why does a crowd of 1,000 protesters make the news anyway? There are more than 300 million people in this country.

I GET TIRED OF CORPORATIONS AND BUSINESSES BEING VILIFIED BY THE MEDIA.

Sorry folks, but those public companies everyone loves to hate are exactly that, publicly-owned companies. This means that a large percentage of ordinary Americans own shares of them via their savings, retirement accounts, and pension funds. When a public company makes good profits, it means better dividends for everyone. And sorry media, when you report the billions in profits that a certain oil company makes in order to make the company look bad, don't forget to report not only the profit number, but also the total sales number. That billion-dollar profit does not look so greedy and evil when you find out it was only a 5 percent profit margin. I would bet that the same media companies have much higher profit margins on average over a period of years than the oil companies.

The media loves to forget that oil companies go through long periods of busts when they make little to no profit, and even years of losses due to the enormous investments they must make to extract that oil that keeps our SUVs running down the road at 75 miles per hour to our kids' next soccer games.

And if we really despise the oil companies so much, then we should act on those convictions and sell our SUVs and switch to horse and buggy! The Amish have managed to do it. And if we really despise the oil companies, we need to quit taking medications, wearing clothes, bandaging our wounds, and seeking medical treatment. There are not too many items in the world that do not contain a petroleum-based product. I hate to break it to everyone, but oil is not an evil, man-made product. It is a completely natural product of our world, and it even seeps naturally into our oceans each and every day.

Why does Wal-Mart get vilified, but Target gets a pass by the media? After all, both stores operate on the same concept of economies of scale to pass on savings to the benefit of their customers. It just seems that everyone loves to hate Wal-Mart.

And why does every network have the same "cloned" female television anchor? They all seem to have bleached blonde hair. We rarely see a brunette. Yet the media is always pushing diversity down our throats.

CHAPTER 8

Organic Food, Environmentalists, and Self-Righteous Celebrities

WHEN DID PEOPLE GET SO SCARED OF THE FOOD THEY EAT?

I love to observe the gullible people who have bought into the organic food craze. It is quite comical to hear these people worry about how our food might kill us, even though people in this country are living longer and longer all the time. I remember when I was a kid that if a person lived to be 80 or 85, we thought that was old. Now, when we read an obituary and see a person that doesn't live to be 90, we think the person died young.

So, I want to ask these paranoid food freaks, "Where are all the people who are dying from our food? My grandma lived to be 95, she never ate an organic food product in her life, and she died of natural causes."

These are the same people that believe cell phones cause brain cancer. Yet no one ever seems to have ever known anyone who ever died of brain cancer from the use of cell phones! And why do people seem to think only brown eggs can be organic, and some people seem to believe that brown eggs are more nutritious? The reason an egg is brown or white is dictated solely by the color of the chicken's feathers. I am sorry folks, but milk is milk; it comes out of the same udder. I worked at a grocery store, and all types of milk came from the same processing plant from the same milk supply; it only had different brand labels at varying prices.

There is no such thing as hormone-free meat folks! Meat has natural hormones from the animal it comes from, and you can't get rid of them.

Self-Righteous Environmentalists and Celebrities

I love the millionaire celebrities who preach to me about how they think people should contribute more in taxes, and they feel that wealthy people should pay more taxes. If you feel so strongly about it, then write a check and make a donation to the government.

Then there are the celebrities who preach about the environment but destroy hundreds of thousands of dollars' worth of materials to make an action movie. They then go home to their 20,000 square foot mansion on the hill and fly about on private jets. Some presidents and politicians preach about the environment, but then they proceed to travel in their motorcades that include countless SUVs and other vehicles. And then there are the celebrities that preach about the wonders of wind power, but do not want wind turbines blocking their view of the ocean from their beachfront homes.

I personally am getting tired of being told that I need to reduce my carbon footprint. If we listen to some of these wacko extremists, they might be happy if I just go out and shoot myself to eliminate my carbon footprint.

Recently, a prince voiced his concerns about overpopulation, the condition of the environment, and global warming.

First of all, "your royal highness," why don't you first donate all of your vast land holdings to conservation? Maybe you could help by having everyone in your royal bloodline stop procreating, so your royal bloodline will go extinct. Speaking of royalty, I also saw a prince announce he and his wife have decided to only have two children to save the planet. How considerate of them! The ego of these people is astounding.

And let's talk about royalty in general here. How in a modern world where everyone… including the royals, claims that all citizens have equality and freedom… can simultaneously subscribe to the belief that somehow these royals have been anointed to rule above everyone else. Who are these people that feel that we must bow in the presence of another human being? The whole notion is medieval and has no place in the modern world.

And now, liberals have managed to make people feel guilty about using plastic straws because they end up in the ocean. I, just one of many consumers of straws, am to blame. Forget about the deadbeats who throw their used straws on the side of the road. So now I have to drink from a paper straw that easily becomes soggy and practically not usable, with my drinks at restaurants.

We now see so-called "health and environmentally-conscious" people attempting to ban hamburgers from certain institutions to protect the planet. These people never rest unless they feel like they can control each and every person.

CHAPTER 9

Religious Contradictions

PEOPLE WHO COME TO CHURCH LATE!

People have reached the height of arrogance when they have no shame in showing up for church services late as if God is waiting for their arrival. Now, we all sometimes arrive to church late. The breed of people I am particularly focused on are the ones who show no modesty or humility when they arrive late. They march down the center aisle so that everyone is aware of their late arrival. The polite and appropriate thing to do is to slip in the back pews or travel down the side aisles so that they can bring the least amount of disruption to the service in progress.

PEOPLE WHO DRESS LIKE SLOBS WHEN THEY COME TO CHURCH

You know who you are, and you all use the same excuse: "God doesn't care so long as I show up." These are the same people who sincerely believe God is the King of Heaven, but the same people wouldn't dream of dressing like this if meeting the Queen of England or President of the United States. These are the same people who sit and listen to the sermon regarding modesty and chastity, but do not even feel embarrassed by the low-cut blouse or short skirt they are wearing in the sanctuary and certainly will never understand the contradiction this combination portrays.

THE LACK OF DECORUM IN CHURCH

This development which has persisted for the last 10 to 15 years is yet another consequence of the "me culture." The last time I went to Christmas Eve Mass, there were people talking while in the communion line. In fact, all through the Mass, there was whispering and even loud talking. The Church teaches that Christ himself is present inside the church building, but we have people talking as if it is some kind of community picnic. When I was a child, I was taught to be silent while inside the Church out of reverence and respect for others. With all the noise inside the Church today, it is becoming more and more difficult to pray and reflect. When things reach this far into the most sacred spaces, our culture is really in trouble.

RAP SINGERS WHO THANK GOD FOR THEIR SUCCESS!

Sorry, rappers, I don't think God approves of your calling women "hoes" and "bitches." I certainly don't think He approves of glorifying violence.

PEOPLE WHO MAKE STUPID COMMENTS WHEN SOMEONE DIES IN AN ACCIDENT

How many times have we heard something like the following? "That car accident was horrible. God called them home." Do these people really think that God decided that people should die in a head-on collision on the highway? If we use the same logic, wouldn't he also decide when a person should be murdered? These are the same people who say, "God was watching over me and saved me from the tornado."

Oh really, so God didn't care about the next-door neighbor, and they were clobbered by flying debris and died? You are so much more important that God saved you for some greater purpose?

WHEN DID CHRISTMAS GET OUT OF CONTROL?

First of all, I am a capitalist and want companies to make money. But retailers have ruined Christmas in this country. Please quit jumping the gun by putting out Christmas decorations in September. Can we please go back to the tradition of starting the Christmas season the day after Thanksgiving? The fun and anticipation have been taken out of the holiday.

And why do people keep falling victim to the political correctness of saying only, "Happy Holidays?" What an absurd ritual many of us have adopted! We all know the holiday we are referring to is Christmas, but we can't actually say the word? The liberals who pretend to be accepting and tolerant and supposedly celebrate our country's "diversity" demonstrate that they are really not tolerant at all. If everyone were truly tolerant, no Christian would be offended by someone who says, "Happy Hanukah" or "Happy Ramadan," nor will any Jew or Muslim be offended by someone who wishes them "Merry Christmas."

It is equivalent to showing up at a party for someone's birthday and instead of saying "happy birthday," we tell them "good morning."

I also find it amusing that everyone runs around all stressed out for two months, shopping and buying things, usually on credit. All to prove they love someone? They then rush around the grocery store the day before Thanksgiving and Christmas to make the perfect dinner. Why are people creating their own self-induced stress?

And now let's talk about the people who act like complete animals by waiting outside all night just to be first in a store to save $5.00 on a pair of shoes. There is something really disturbing about people who mob the door to Target at 5 a.m. the day after Thanksgiving. There is no place for it in a civilized society. Let's stop and look at ourselves and ask ourselves, "What example are we setting for our children by acting this way?"

After all, the word "Christmas" is a derivation of the words "Christ's Mass." If we really look at the behavior and activities most typically associated with Christmas, they are far removed from the message of the person that lends His name to the holiday.

WHEN DID HALLOWEEN BECOME SUCH A BIG HOLIDAY?

For such a Christian nation as America, it certainly amazes me that so many people get so caught up in Halloween, which is a holiday based on ancient pagan and superstitious beliefs, but more recently it is tied to honoring the Christian dead. Today's Halloween is a mere secular occasion. And what is with these silly parents who insist on dressing up their babies and taking them trick-or-treating? Really, a one-year-old is going to have fun on Halloween?

And for you adults that dress up all day at work, Halloween really is a secular kid's holiday, so grow up!

What is with Halloween greeting cards? Why would I wish someone a Happy Halloween when its origins are based on remembering the dead?

THE POPE AND WALLS

Then we have the blatant contradictory statements of the Pope, who criticizes the U.S. President's plan to build a wall to keep out illegal aliens from our country. The Pope lives inside the world's smallest independent country which is surrounded on all sides by a very tall wall and guards with medieval weapons at the ready.

I am sure some of my staunch Catholic relatives are going to be praying for me for sharing this opinion.

FUNDAMENTALIST CHRISTIANS WHO OBSESS ABOUT THE END OF THE WORLD

We are all going to die someday. So basically, everyone will face their own "end of the world." So, what difference does it make if for some reason we all die at the same time? And you know what else? If the actual world does someday come to an end, which it will… because the sun isn't going to burn forever, then we can just quit worrying about it. There isn't a damn thing we can do to stop it.

CHAPTER 10

Politicians and the So-called Ruling Class

I am increasingly alarmed by our so-called "Ruling Class" in this country, the United States of America. Based on what I have observed from our Congressional leaders over the last three years, I believe that we are in extreme danger as a country. Some of the things these people say are becoming increasingly irrational all the time.

Twenty years ago, if someone suggested something as ignorant and irrational as the "Green New Deal," those people would have been laughed off as idiots. Now, we have everyone taking these people seriously. Are we becoming a nation where we let uneducated fools dictate our path ahead?

Are Americans going to ever wake up to the lies and disease of gullibility these politicians spread throughout our country? Don't people ever question why we keep talking about the same old national problems for decades and decades? Well, we have to take a look at how many politicians serve in Congress over and over. Many have for decades and decades. Are we to believe that in the last 40 years they couldn't solve our looming issues with social security and immigration?

I have only been around since 1972, but I can remember the same problems presented to the American people over and over. And of course, there is always an urgent crisis regarding an issue, yet no one can fix it. We are usually told that we have only so long before catastrophe, but then the politicians move onto the next scare tactic and leave the current catastrophe for another generation to recycle again in a few years.

The way politicians talk about taxation in this country is as if they have the unfettered right to decide how much of our money we get to keep. They pit one social class against another to manipulate our tax laws to the benefit of shaping voter blocks that will keep getting them reelected. It is an evil and deceptive game these politicians play on the American people. The politicians constantly reward certain groups with special exceptions to the tax policies.

We now have approximately 44% of American households who do not contribute a dime to the federal taxes because they "qualify" for the earned income credit, and that is just because they have families of a certain size and Congress has decided that aspect warrants special privileges. A group of people who use the most of our resources in the country contribute absolutely nothing.

The politicians spout off that the rich are not paying their fair share while 44% of Americans contribute absolutely nothing. The concept of taxation is that everyone should contribute to the common good and provide things that can only occur collectively. As an overly-taxed citizen, I am angered that these citizens who do not contribute continue to have such a loud voice and say in how things are done in this country. But wait, it proves my point! These 44% of non-taxpaying citizens are voting for someone, aren't they?

I am further appalled at how many ignorant politicians keep getting elected, who call America a democracy. We are not a democracy. We are a democratic republic, with representative government. Some call it a democratic constitutional republic. Read the Constitution. America was founded upon the principle that the state's rights should take precedence over federal control. This concept is clearly demonstrated in the brilliant concept of the Electoral College that so many uneducated politicians are now demanding that we eliminate. These fools keep complaining over and over when a president wins the electoral vote, but not the popular vote, as if it is an anomaly. When a candidate wins the election via the electoral vote, it is happening just as it was intended.

POLITICIANS WHO ARE DESCRIBED AS PUBLIC SERVANTS

Sorry, but they get paid and at a higher rate than the average taxpayer. They then receive a full pension after very little time spent in office at the expense of the public. Sorry, they are paid employees, and overpaid ones at that. Most of them should be called "Public Mooches."

I especially enjoy the senator who lives his life in office stating he believes in the right to have an abortion. Then at his funeral mass, a cardinal of the Catholic Church not only says the Mass, but then allows an eloquent eulogy to be delivered that one would think the Senator is a "saint."

I have an idea. If we as a people really want to solve the corruption problem in Washington, then we should insist on a balanced budget and congressional term limits. I also believe we should establish by law that no one elected to federal office should be qualified to receive any kind of pension. This would eliminate the career politicians who entrench themselves and look after their own by secretly securing lucrative benefits for themselves even years after leaving office.

And why do we need to pay to keep former presidents with offices around the country, after their terms are completed? I also don't believe it is necessary to provide secret service protection for people for more than 10 years after leaving office. Most of these former politicians milked the taxpayers enough while in office, so why not let them use their profits from their fictionalized self-written accounts of their years in office, called memoirs and pay for their own security? Does anyone really believe that a president who left office in 1981 is really a target for someone anymore?

And what is the need for these presidential libraries? They seem more like self-glorified propaganda to help shape opinions regarding presidential legacies.

POLITICIANS WHO KISS BABIES AND WAVE TO PHANTOM FRIENDS IN THE CROWD

Do people really make their decision to vote for people based on this silliness? Do we really believe Hillary Clinton was waving to a long lost friend in the crowd on the tour?

CITIZENS WHO BLINDLY SUPPORT POLITICIANS

I find it hard to understand how anyone can become so invested in any elected official. They blindly support a certain candidate through thick and thin, with the loyalty that should only be reserved for a spouse! They are quite a strange breed of people. Do they really think that candidate is loyal to them?

I found it humorous to watch all the people in tears because Hillary Clinton did not get elected president. Really! Do they really think their lives are going to change that much based on just one presidential election? And likewise to the others who are so distraught that Trump won. Is he really going to be able to change lives that much? How do we go through each day putting so much faith in one person as if he or she is going to make lives better? Only we can control the quality of our lives.

Some candidates have won over the years that I didn't like, but I never obsessed over it like these people who hate Trump so much. Deal with it. He is the elected president.

What is with people who blindly support a presidential candidate who promises he will do this or that? Read the Constitution. These presidential candidates often promise to do things they have no constitutional authority to fulfill. Everyone seems so focused on how important it is to have the right president in office. But look at some of the idiots in Congress. The public seems to elect over and over some of the biggest idiots in history to Congress. And Congress really has the most power to do the most damage to our lives.

It is so obvious from the tweets, posts and commentary of our news media that an alarmingly large number of American citizens have never even glanced at our Constitution. What a beautifully simple document if we would just read, discuss, understand and follow it! I can tell very quickly when the media and other people reference our government as a "democracy," that they don't even understand our own system of government. To set the record straight, we are a democratic republic, not a democracy.

ENFORCEMENT OF LAWS IS NOW CONTROVERSIAL.

Our society is really breaking down when we have blatant disregard for the rule of law demonstrated by elected officials. It is now racist and controversial to enforce our immigration laws? Some of the same people who criticize the president for enforcing our immigration laws are members of Congress, who passed the actual immigration laws in question. The president is constitutionally required to enforce and has the right to sign all laws passed by Congress. The majority of Americans have no problem with immigration so long as it is controlled and legal. Most people know we need immigration to meet the growing needs of a healthy economy, but it has to be controlled. Most Americans want immigrants who love our country and who contribute to our society. People typically don't let just anyone off the streets into their houses, so why are so many demanding that America just open her doors to everyone and anyone?

WHY DO I HAVE TO PRESENT AN ID TO BUY BEER, BUT THERE ARE PEOPLE WHO PREACH ABOUT HOW IT IS RACIST AND UNREASONABLE FOR SOMEONE TO HAVE TO PROVE THEIR ELIGIBILITY TO VOTE BY SHOWING AN ID?

I have to ask, why is this even allowed to be presented as a legitimate concern? Shouldn't we all be concerned that anyone without an ID can potentially not be qualified to vote? In the same regard, why are people who insist that the President prove his eligibility to run for office portrayed as some extremists or wacky people? After all, the President is only going to be the Commander in Chief of our military. I think the founders were pretty brilliant in their requirement that only a natural born citizen could serve as President.

Imagine what would happen if an enemy of our country, went through the motions to become a citizen, was elected as President, and then took advantage of that position as Commander in Chief in a traitorous act?

STUPID LIQUOR LAWS!

Some states including the ones I am most familiar with, Oklahoma and Texas, have some of the stupidest liquor laws anywhere. For example, we cannot buy beer after 1 a.m. in a convenience store in certain cities, but we can go right down the street and continue to buy alcohol and drink it inside a bar until 2 a.m. and then drive home. Now who is most likely to drive drunk? The person who has been at the bar drinking until 2 a.m. or the person who hasn't drunk anything but buys the beer at 2 a.m. to take home and then drink it?

ALL POLITICIANS AND MEDIA GET IT WRONG WHEN DEBATING GUN CONTROL AND THE RIGHT TO BEAR ARMS!

Folks, our founders did not insert the second amendment because they were worried about crime prevention. It was included as the ultimate check and balance on a tyrannical government. I find it so aggravating that no one in the debates ever brings up that the main point of the right to bear arms is to preserve and protect our ultimate freedom! The second amendment is quite brilliant and a very simple concept. It does not require lengthy debate and complicated legal analysis.

To the people who want to ban all guns… guns don't kill people; people do as we have seen in other nations with extreme gun laws. If someone really wants to kill another person, they will find a way, whether by using a car, a bomb, poison, or a knife. Do we say someone's hands killed someone when they strangle someone? So why do these people insist on saying that guns kill people?

Who are these liberal people that think because they stick a poster on the wall that says, "Gun-free Zone," that a criminal is going to abide by it? How many people each and every day ignore the speed limit sign on the highway?

POLITICIANS WHO CREATED THE PROBLEMS AND THEN PROCLAIM TO BE THE ONES WHO CAN SOLVE THEM!

I especially despise these devious types of politicians who spend thirty years in office and blame some program they previously condoned but that has expanded and gotten out of control. These same politicians voted for the program that is causing the problem and then have the audacity to claim they will now solve the problem.

HOW MANY MORE LAWS OR REGULATIONS COULD WE POSSIBLY NEED?

Don't we think after more than 232 years, we have probably covered just about everything? I mean murder is murder. Do we really need hate crimes laws?

After all murder is still murder and is offensive and disgusting no matter who was killed. I would love to see Congress just take a few years off and leave the rest of us alone. Of course, this will require a constitutional amendment. I bet anyone anything, life would get better. Why do people think we need a Congress that continually finds new laws to pass that make something that was legal today illegal tomorrow?

IF OUR GOVERNMENT FINDS CIGARETTES SO DANGEROUS, THEN WHY HAVEN'T THEY OUTLAWED THEM?

Simple, because the government does not care a wink about our health! The cigarette industry is just another means for government to extort large amounts of money out of the private sector. The government keeps it legal, while requiring large taxes on the product. Then the saps that produce the cigarettes are preyed upon by lawyers to obtain settlements for people who bought the cigarettes, even though there was a clearly marked label warning them of the dangers of using the product.

PEOPLE WHO SAY, "THE GOVERNMENT WILL PAY FOR IT."

I especially love the ignorant people who make that statement. It never occurs to them where the government gets the money. People who make that comment can only be people who don't actually contribute and pay a tax bill each year. They are happy to mooch off the backs of their hardworking, tax-paying neighbors and fellow citizens.

WHY DO PEOPLE WHO DON'T PAY INCOME TAXES STILL GET TO VOTE?

This may seem an outrageous thing to say, but there was a very logical reason why there used to be laws requiring that a person should own property in order to be able to vote. After all, why should someone who does not contribute toward the common good have an equal say in how the fruits of others get allocated? Now, these laws existed before the annual income tax, but the same logic should apply today for those who don't pay federal taxes. If there ever was a need for a constitutional amendment, this is one. Wake up, people. Once the majority of people voting, and we are probably already there, are the same ones not paying taxes, God help us. The burden-bearers of society who work and pay taxes are becoming enslaved to a new class of masters. These masters are happy to sit back and milk the public coffers without contributing a thing. It is just another version of slavery.

WHY DOES GOD ONLY EXPECT ME TO TITHE 10 %, BUT SOME POLITICIANS FEEL ENTITLED TO 30 % OF THE FRUITS OF MY LABOR?

Sorry, Mr. Politician, but I am paying more than my fair share!

Why, because I am single, has our government decided I should contribute a higher percentage of my income in taxes?

I have no children utilizing the school system. I only own one vehicle that I drive on the highway system. I am supposed to believe it is my obligation to subsidize the users of the school system and other government services.

RACISM ACCUSATIONS ARE SLANDEROUS.

I hate to break it to people, but just because someone is critical of or disagrees with anyone who is considered a minority… this does not make the critic or debater a racist. Of course, there are bigoted and racist people. However, I don't buy the repeated line that America in general is a racist country. If America were truly as racist as some complain, then Barak Obama would not have been elected twice to the presidency.

I MISS THE GREATEST GENERATION.

I don't know about everyone else, but I sure do miss having the Greatest Generation in charge of running our country. Back in the days of Reagan, the last time I could say I felt confident, the right people with the right attitude were in charge of our government institutions. Even though there were both Republicans and Democrats who were part of the Greatest Generation, it seemed that every one of them conducted themselves with more honor, decorum, and decency than now… even during disagreements.

Today, we have petty and childish bickering among Republicans and Democrats while our country slips into ruination. Of course, politics have always been laced with partisan thinking, but not to the extent it is today. Petty arguments about frivolous issues are replacing serious and dignified debate. Can you imagine a presidential campaign only 20 years ago, where so-called serious candidates for the presidency would have resorted to alluding to another candidate's penis size? Of course, we shouldn't be surprised. I find it ironic that the so-called news media has the gall to act surprised, when they are usually the same people who mock conservatives or liberals who voice concern about such crudities being injected into so-called family television news and shows.

Say what you will, but those people just 20 years ago who warned us about the deterioration of common decency were right. Little by little, as crude and obscene language and culture have been allowed to become mainstream, they are now revealed in the most hallowed of national institutions.

CHAPTER 11

Stupid People Everywhere!

The self-centered "me" culture that has promulgated on American society for the last 20 years manifests itself profoundly throughout our culture. People in this country are now allowed and even encouraged to act out their ignorance on the general public.

THE HYPERSENSITIVE AND THE EASILY OFFENDED CROWD

First of all, if you fall under this category, the first thing I have to say is… get a sense of humor and grow up! What is with this new phenomenon of "safe spaces?" I would have thought the term "safe space" was reserved for such things as tornado or bomb shelters. But really, people, safe spaces from speech and even ideas?

These current college students, who can't even handle free speech without breaking down, are in for a real wake-up call when they leave the "utopia" of their college "safe space" and find themselves in the middle of things called "life" and "reality." These protected ones are going to be in for a surprise when their employer is not really concerned about their feelings but wants to know why they are not performing effectively on the job.

I hate to break it to these weak and wimpy college graduates, but there are several billion other people on the planet, and they just may occasionally have beliefs and ideas that don't always mesh with theirs.

PROTESTERS!

Can any so-called protester even name one person they have ever convinced to change a mind because they decided to throw a temper tantrum and shut down the city streets, while inconveniencing everyone else? By the way, everyone has the right to protest in this country. Everyone can protest every few years. It is called a ballot.

I especially enjoy the irony of the Dakota Access Pipeline opponents who protest for "environmental reasons" but then go on to leave tons of garbage that pollute the ground and potentially the river nearby. There are similar examples of protesters who leave tons of litter on the National Lawn in Washington D.C. after one of their little temper tantrums.

If you really think about it, protesters don't really respect free speech or their fellow Americans. Protesting is really a form of coercion to compel others to act differently. Lately, the protesters act more like a rioting mob that threatens people. They do change behavior through coercion because they usually create an inconvenience for others.

WHY CAN'T PEOPLE MERGE INTO TRAFFIC PROPERLY?

We see the following on a regular basis: the freeway traffic is flowing smoothly until someone needs to merge into traffic. Then it all goes to hell in a few seconds. It wouldn't go to hell if a majority of people would revisit some basic traffic rules that we all should have learned when we earned our driver's licenses.

First, the traffic on the freeway has the right of way, and the people merging from the ramp are supposed to yield to the freeway traffic. However, it seems that the majority of people have it mixed up, and they think this rule is reversed. What do they do? They race up the ramp and either nearly crash into the freeway traffic or pull out in front of them and make everyone slow down unnecessarily.

Second, merging into traffic is not complicated! If you are merging into traffic from the on-ramp, you simply either adjust your speed up or down so that you can merge seamlessly into the traffic. And don't give me that dirty look because I didn't slow down for you. Either speed up fast enough to get in front of me without interrupting my speed, or slow down and fall in behind me.

What is this business of people who think they have to swerve in front of me if I am in the fast lane, and they are in the right lane when they see someone stopped on the shoulder? There is a reason state governments contract out to build the interstate highways with shoulders! They are built so the two or more lanes on the freeways can keep moving even if someone is changing a tire on the side of the road. If we feel the need to merge into the fast lane when passing someone who is parked on the shoulder, the same rules apply. We must do it in a way that doesn't result in making those in the fast lane slow down and maybe even causing them to slam on breaks.

And what is with these people who act like they are driving a semi-trailer truck when making a turn in a compact car? When making a turn from one lane, the driver doesn't need to first move partially into another lane to start the turn. Trust me. Unless the driver is hauling a load of freight in a Peterbilt-type vehicle, the driver will clear the curb.

GAWKERS ON THE HIGHWAY

How many times have we all been in a major traffic jam for half an hour or more? Then when we finally get up to where the delay originated, it is because of a wreck on the other side of the road. What is so interesting that people have to slow down for a wreck on the other side? I think a large number of these gawkers are hoping to see a dead body or something.

PEOPLE WHO ACT SURPRISED WHEN THEIR BEACHFRONT HOME WASHES AWAY

Sorry, but that is the risk of building a house on the beach. And since the property owner is likely a wealthy person to be able to own a house on the beach in the first place, then that person should deal with it without complaining to the rest of us who must live in our modest inland homes.

PEOPLE WHO ACT SURPRISED WHEN NEW ORLEANS FLOODS DURING A HURRICANE

So, let me get this right. A large part of the city sits below sea level. Why the surprise when it floods?

PEOPLE WHO THINK LAS VEGAS IS THE NEXT BEST THING

I have been to Vegas, and no one could pay me or bribe me with a free trip to ever go back. The Vegas Strip is nothing but a superficial, glorified shopping mall. I am amazed at the marketing genius of the executives who can convince gullible and shallow people to spend money flying to a desert landscape where it is 115° F outside and at the same time, convince the same people that hotel rooms are free, while those people shell out money hand over fist to gamble and for food and drink at exorbitant prices. Bravo to the marketing genius working for the gaming industry!

WHY DOES IT TAKE SO LONG FOR PEOPLE TO BOARD AN AIRCRAFT?

What is the complicating factor of boarding an airplane that makes people take so long to find a seat? We see it all the time. Everyone acts like they have never seen an airplane. It is simple. We walk down the aisle and place our luggage in an overhead compartment and sit down.

CLUELESS PEOPLE WHO INSIST ON USING THE SELF CHECKOUT LINE AT THE GROCERY STORE

In the 21st Century, I am amazed by the idiots who use the self checkout line and act as if it is their first encounter with such technology. Folks, it wasn't invented as a novelty for us to explore like a work of art. It is designed for speedy checkout.

To these people, I request, "Do the rest of us a favor. If you are not smart enough to follow both written and voice prompted instructions, that simply require you to push a few buttons, then please go to the old-fashioned line where someone can do it for you."

CHAPTER 12

Can We Be Honest?

WHY CAN'T PEOPLE STATE THINGS FOR WHAT THEY REALLY ARE?

Why do people insist on calling toilet paper "bathroom tissue?" Why is the toilet... the restroom? I certainly never see a couch in the toilet at the office building to rest upon. Why do people insist on saying someone passes away when the person has died? Did the person just magically vanish into thin air? Graveyards were suddenly called "cemeteries," but now are politely called "memorial gardens." When did politicians' lies become known as prevarications? When did a zero rate of spending growth become known as a budget cut? When did "becoming old" become a negative thing that requires us to restate the condition as "advanced age?" Why do we call juvenile jails, "juvenile justice centers?" It makes it sound like the kids there are the ones that need protection from society instead of society being protected from them. In the same way, we now call criminal courts… the "criminal justice system." We have renamed "progressive discipline" as "progressive coaching!" Why do we call "you're fired…" "termination of employment?"

WHY ARE WOMEN CONSIDERED A DISADVANTAGED CLASS?

Women account for 50.8 percent of the United States population. Women have had the right to vote in this country since 1920. So why are women considered a minority group?

The feminists claim that they are equal to men, but if they account for a majority of the population and have the right to vote, then the only reason for their secondary prominence in society must be that they are not equal to men or are too lazy to vote. They really can't have it both ways. Or I would argue that they are really not as disadvantaged as some may claim.

I really don't buy that women cannot make it in the corporate world. In my career I have answered to as many women as men who were either my boss or in a superior position to my own.

SORRY, THERE REALLY IS A DIFFERENCE BETWEEN MEN AND WOMEN.

And now for the politically incorrect truth, there is a difference between men and women. Unfortunately, our society has turned these differences into political war instead of just acknowledging that men and women have unique inherent traits, both good and bad. I think most men affectionately consider most women to be a totally different species. Likewise, many women consider men to be Neanderthals.

We all know that typically women react more by emotions than men do. And it is true, men really don't grow up. We just enjoy more expensive toys such as motorboats, motorcycles, and guns.

And sorry, but women are not biologically as strong as men and cannot be considered equal to the task when it comes to armed combat in the military.

CHAPTER 13

Some Other Things That Really Annoy Me

WHEN DID TIPPING GET OUT OF CONTROL?

Don't get me wrong. I have worked as a valet parker and as a waiter and know the importance of tipping. People who work in fields where tipping is common should also demonstrate graciousness when receiving tips, not entitlement.

But wait a minute. I am not going to tip the guy at the sandwich shop for making my sandwich. Especially, since I must first stand in line and wait for some dimwit to make the sandwich, then wait in line to pay for it, get my own cup, then fill my own cup, get my own napkin, and then when I am through eating, have to clean my own table and throw away the trash. Anyone who tips in this situation is a moron.

ANIMAL RIGHTS HYPOCRITES

It really amazes me that people are ready to rake the CEO of a major airline over the coals for the accidental death of a dog on a flight. However, many of these people who are so concerned remain silent when people deliberately kill unborn human babies on a daily basis in this country. And does the accidental death of a dog on an airline really justify having a breaking news banner?

OVERLY FANCY RESTAURANTS

Ok, I cringe when a waiter asks, "Have you dined with us before?" First of all, your restaurant is not that unique that I need a detailed introduction about what you are doing. I especially hate steak houses that think they need to provide me a diagram and history of the different cuts of beef on the menu. And what is it with steak houses that get offended because I ask for a well-done steak? And then they further insult me by telling me that they won't guarantee the steak will be exactly well-done, and that it will take longer to cook. Most people know that to get the steak well-done, the chef must leave it on the fire longer. And lastly I am paying for it and I am the customer. So why can't they just say, "Certainly," and be done with it?

Please… will they spare me with the fancy presentation of their "proprietary filtered water" in a fancy vase. It is tap water, not champagne!

Waiters must realize I have the greatest respect for them as I know how hard their jobs can be and they are often underestimated. But they must learn the difference between friendly service and too personal of service. Just because I am polite and friendly and even smile, does not mean I want to know the waiter's life story. I am usually dining out and am interested in the company I have with me, not the waiter's company.

Please, let's stop this trend where waiters sit down across from us to take our order. It does not feel personal. It is often quite an awkward moment for the customer on the receiving end of this "new custom." Please, servers should not ask me if I want change. They should assume I do. No one likes to be given hints about the tip that should be given. Servers should not ask me if I want an iced tea refill when my glass is empty, and I have just gotten my food. Of course, I want a refill. And the worst offense with fancy restaurants is when they bring out a beautifully garnished hamburger and fries and do not automatically bring ketchup to the table. And then they think it is ok to make us wait 5 minutes to get the condiment we asked for, so we have to wait to begin eating.

When I am dining alone, I ask that restaurant hosts please stop asking me if I want to sit in the bar. I know the bar is always open seating. So… if I tell the host or hostess that there is just one person, it is obvious that I would like to be seated like everyone else.

And what is with this practice of seating me right next to other people when the restaurant is almost empty? Servers should give us all a little space until they need those tables during busy times.

CAN RESTAURANTS PLEASE QUIT SERVING MASHED POTATOES WITH THE SKINS?

Please, chefs of the world, show some courage to break away from this annoying trend. Can I just have simple mashed potatoes that have been completely peeled, with nothing more than cream, butter, salt and pepper?

I AM TIRED OF BUSINESSES ASKING ME TO COMPLETE A SURVEY!

I get sick of being asked to complete some stupid online survey every time I purchase something at a store. Some stores are so obsessive about it that your receipt is a foot long just for buying a pack of paper clips. How about this idea? Why don't they ask their managers to visit with and get to know us customers while we are in the store?

WHY DOES IT SEEM EVERYONE HAS A HANDICAP PLACARD?

They know who they are. They are the ones who are not really that disabled but still display and use their handicap placard like it is a badge of honor or something. I love watching the people with these placards as they park and sprint into the mall. I am convinced that the only handicap some of these people have is brain damage.

These people are about as brain-damaged as the people who circle the mall for 20 minutes trying to find a parking space close to the entrance and finally find a close space, get out and then, only to walk for miles around the mall all afternoon.

PEOPLE WHO LOOK DOWN ON THE SO-CALLED LITTLE PEOPLE

Sorry folks, but not everyone gets the chance in life to live like a celebrity and make millions of dollars. Take the time to say, "Hello," to the maid or janitor. After all, they are willing to clean up everyone else's crap. And I literally mean crap.

How many times do people walk by these people without so much as making eye-to-eye contact to even acknowledge these people as human beings?

I really love watching the silly British when they worry so much about what social class someone belongs to, or whether people have a title in front of their name. There are two equalizers in life. We all poop, and we all die. Even the Queen of England sometimes gets the "runs." When we look at it that way, does someone's title really matter all that much?

WHEN DID TATTOOS BECOME A MUST HAVE-ITEM FOR EVERYONE?

When I was growing up, the only people who got tattoos were sailors and bikers. Now, everyone follows the crowd and seems to have one. I always counsel young people to not get a visible tattoo. If people ignore that advice, then they shouldn't be surprised when they don't get promoted up the corporate ladder.

Likewise, what is with these people who get these disgusting piercings on their lips and eyebrows? It sure looks painful. It is especially unappetizing to look at when these pierced people are bagging my groceries.

CHILD BEAUTY PAGEANTS

It takes just one word to describe this phenomenon. Creepy! What is it with people who want to treat their young daughters like dress up dolls and paint them with makeup and make them look like little miniature drag queens? It is sick and disgusting and truly one of the most bizarre activities to be found anywhere on the planet.

THE RUNNING OF THE BULLS IN SPAIN

This is certainly one of the most idiotic things in our modern world. It is not because I am an animal rights activist. I just think people who participate in this are plain brain dead for putting their lives in danger for no good reason.

BLESSING SOMEONE WHO SNEEZES!

I am really going to be called the Grinch for this thought. But I really get tired of someone saying, "Bless you," when I sneeze. And then I get scolded as if I am rude for not saying my obligatory, "Thank you," after their supposed blessing.

What am I thanking them for? Are they God and did they really bless me? I mean it is just a body function to expel foreign material from my nose. And why do they say, "Bless you," instead of… "May God bless you?"

SELF-RIGHTEOUS EUROPEANS

I really get sick of Europeans lecturing America on our flaws and our place in the world. These are countries who have as their legacy World War I and II, Hitler, Mussolini, and the Holocaust.

WHY DO BUILDERS TRY TO ELIMINATE THE 13TH FLOOR OF A BUILDING?

Builders can take the number 13 off the registry of building floors and list the 14th floor as the one immediately following the 12th floor. But guess what? There still is a 13th floor in the building, and it is the 14th floor. The only way they can eliminate the 13th floor is to build a building no taller than 12 floors high.

I have purposely made this book to include 13 chapters and included the above in the 13th chapter just to be ornery.

SORRY, BUT EUROPE IS NOT THE BEST PLACE IN THE WORLD TO LIVE!

I get so sick of people comparing America to Europe. I have lived and visited overseas, and I can tell you from personal experience, America is the best place to live. Of course, most people think their home country is the best place. Anyone who likes giving up over 50 percent of their earnings to the State, then by all means, they should go to Europe. If anyone likes paying $12 per gallon for gasoline, then by all means, go live there. If people don't like being able to afford heating the entire house, but instead heat only a few rooms and wear a sweater the whole time they are indoors, then by all means, they should move to Europe. If people think eating a steak should always be an extravagant luxury, then they should go live in Europe and find out how much that steak costs.

There is a cost to that romantic way of living in Europe with their two-month vacations and spare time to sit in cafes drinking coffee. It's called high taxes.

PEOPLE OBSESSIVELY TAKING PHOTOGRAPHS ON VACATION!

Vacationers should put the stupid camera down and take a moment to actually enjoy the place they are visiting. They should quit asking strangers to take pictures for them. Strangers are not their private family photographers. Oh, and the people who walk around hiking in the mountains with a camera stick are the most ridiculous anywhere. I even saw where one of these people ended up getting struck by lightning because he was hiking in a thunderstorm with the camera stick held up high.

People who take their so-called "selfies." Can anyone be any more narcissistic? It is getting so bad that people are now taking "selfies" at sacred sites such as former concentration camps. I recently saw a guy lie down on the street in Dallas, where "X" marks the spot of Kennedy's assassination… to pose for a photo while laughing and acting silly. Visiting the site of someone's murder inspires them to laughter, instead of dignified reflection?

WHY DO PEOPLE ACT STUPID WHEN IT COMES TO DOUBLE DOOR ENTRIES?

We see it all the time. There are double doors to enter a building, but everyone acts like they must cram through one of them instead of opening and using the second door also. The double doors are very conducive to two-way traffic if people would simply open the second door. These are the same people who always manage to stop to have a conversation right at the bottom of an escalator or a doorway, keeping others from being able to use either.

The same people walk with their friends down the sidewalk and somehow find a way to hog the entire sidewalk and don't even bother to move over, but make me and others move over and have to walk into the grass as we try to pass them. Can't we share the sidewalk? By the way, since we are in America and we drive on the right side of the road, the same logic… walking on the ride side of any path… should apply to two-way pedestrian traffic on the sidewalk.

WHY DO NEWS REPORTERS ALWAYS MANAGE TO FIND THE MOST IGNORANT EYE WITNESS TO INTERVIEW?

We see it all the time. News reporters interview someone who witnessed a particular crime. They always seem to have most of their teeth missing and can't complete a full sentence and fail to use proper grammar. Even worse, is when the news reporter interviews a child, as if they can form an intelligent opinion at 10 years of age?

PEOPLE WHO ACT CONFUSED ABOUT A FAST FOOD MENU!

Seriously, how many times have we been to fast food restaurants in our lives, and some of us don't pretty much know what is typically on the menus? These people wait in line for 20 minutes, the whole time standing in front of a 5 ft. by 5 ft. menu on the wall. Then when it is their turn, they try to decide what they want. On top of that, they act like they are in a fine dining restaurant by making their special requests to hold this or that or put extra onions on the burger. I also love the people who order the supersized burger and fries, which total about 2,000 calories and then ask for the Diet Coke.

WHY IS THERE NO "INFLUENZA AWARENESS" RIBBON?

Why do some diseases command greater sympathy and honor than others? Don't get me wrong. Cancer can result in a horrible death. But why are cancer victims always portrayed as if they fought in Iwo

Jima and deserve the Purple Heart? But if someone dies of the old-fashioned flu, no fuss is ever made about the death. All of these millions and millions of dollars spent over the last 30 years to find a cure for cancer, only to produce no cure. We never have a fundraiser for the flu victims who die each year. Yes, millions of people die each year from cancer. But why are their deaths more tragic than the ones who die of the flu, choking, or of natural causes for that matter? My point is to keep the recognition of diseases and illnesses in perspective. We all die at some point. Regardless of the cause of death, the end of a loved one's life usually results in survivors who grieve, and the cause, at that point, does not really matter.

ROADSIDE MEMORIALS

I have relatives that died in car accidents, but my family didn't build a private memorial on the side of the road to commemorate the spots where they each died.

How selfish are people to think that their loved one deserves to have a private memorial for all perpetuity on the side of a public highway. Why do they make the tractor driver's job more difficult by putting him in the difficult position of trying not to damage the private memorial while mowing the right of way? A lot of these memorials mark the spot where some drunk ended his or her life and maybe even the lives of others by wrecking a car. Not really an honorable thing worthy of a memorial!

People die in all kinds of places, including hotel rooms, restaurants, and offices all the time. If we use the same logic, we would have restaurant tables, hotel rooms, and office suites put out of commission to commemorate the site of people's deaths.

HISTORICAL PRESERVATIONISTS!

Don't get me wrong. I like history and historic sites. But what is with these people who insist on government subsidies to preserve technology, buildings, and services for nostalgia's sake even when they are outdated and not economical in today's world. These are the people who want to spend millions bringing back trolleys to downtown cities for a small five-block run, when a person can walk the five blocks faster than a wait for the limited connections on the "nostalgic trolley."

I especially resent the "preservationists" who want to dictate what other people do with their own private property. These hipster historians establish committees and commissions which become filled with stupid power-hungry people who dictate what others can build or tear down on their own residential and business properties. If anyone wants to preserve something, that is fine, but they should do it with their own money on their own property. If they don't want a neighbor to tear down a "historic home," then the best idea is to make them a fair offer and buy it from them. Then, the new owner can do anything with the property!

Recently, a good Denver man's retirement plans were nearly destroyed by a bunch of self-righteous preservationists that found a way to slap his property with a historic preservation restriction. This kept him from selling his property at its full value so he could retire. I cannot imagine how angry I would be if something like that had happened to me. These people talk as if they own his property and that he should come to them to work out a solution that works for everyone. How in America can we allow such individuals the power to take something away so casually from a man who put in his sweat and blood over many years to build his own retirement? How did these preservationists earn a chair at this man's table? Fortunately, the restriction was reversed, and he can now sell his property as originally planned. How many more people like him though, have not been as fortunate?

RIGHTERS OF WRONGS OF THE PAST!

I am so tired of self-righteous people who impose today's morality on the morality of 200 years ago. These are the people who always preach how we should apologize for this or that. One of their "pet" causes is to get the United States to apologize for dropping the first atom bomb on Japan. How about first demanding the Japanese to apologize for the damage they caused to the world and the millions of people they are responsible for killing?

I really love the self-righteous people who say we should give the American Indians their land back.

Ok, if you believe that, then start the movement by deeding over your home to the tribe that historically inhabited the land your house stands on today. There isn't a house in the United States today, that doesn't stand on land once inhabited by American Indians. Where do we draw the line? Where does the responsibility begin and end for the wrongs of the past? Exactly how many generations must come and go before the score can be settled?

THE UNITED STATES POSTAL SERVICE DOES NOT DESERVE NOSTALGIC PROTECTION.

I love to hear the people who work for the post office complain about how bad it is to work there and how the postal service keeps losing money. It's not hard to figure out why they are failing. Ever been to most post offices today? What do you usually find? I will tell you. It is often a grumpy, lazy and extremely slow and inept person working the counter. They have three speeds; (1) when it is not busy slow; (2) when it gets a little busy slow; (3) when they are very busy and there is a line of 30 people waiting to buy stamps, still slow! I have no sympathy for the predicament of the postal service when we get service like this. And this is so typical of anything the government runs. Not to mention that the postal service is becoming more and more obsolete now that most people use email!

And why do politicians feel the need to bail out this institution? Some do simply because of its heritage. If heritage is so important for an obsolete business to remain in business, then why not bring back the Pony Express? Actually that may not be such a bad idea as the Pony Express was in fact faster than current modern day postal service. And what is with the people in line who spend five minutes discussing which stamp to buy? What the hell difference does it make whether to buy a commemorative stamp or just a basic stamp? It is just postage! Do we really know anyone who gets that impressed with the stamp we put on the envelope?

I AM TIRED OF SMALL TOWN "MAIN STREET" BUSINESS OWNERS THAT COMPLAIN ABOUT HOW DIFFICULT IT IS TO STAY IN BUSINESS.

First of all, businesses must compete which means each must sell things that people actually need. They must also face reality and acknowledge that a town's main street isn't really the "main street" anymore but is now the interstate highway on the other side of town. Then, they need to be open for business at times that are convenient for the potential customers. Some of these Main Street business owners adopt business hours that are more reminiscent of a bygone era, often even closing on Saturdays. How do they expect to sell anything when they are closed on the one day a week most potential customers have time to actually shop?

BUSINESSES THAT DON'T TAKE CREDIT CARDS!

Ok, we all have to get with the modern times. We have to quit claiming it is too expensive to take credit cards in our small stores. We should do what everyone else does and incorporate the cost of credit card transactions into the pricing. All the other stores absorb it and pass it on to their customers. They just don't whine and complain about it being the 21st Century.

WHY DO SOME WEALTHY PEOPLE HAVE TO PRETEND THEY ARE POOR?

I have nothing against anyone who has been successful or even lucky in order to have material wealth. But what is it with some people in that position who go out of their way to pretend and complain about how tough they have it? This is especially common among farmers and ranchers who own several thousand acres of land with oil wells dotting the landscape, while they get into their $50,000 ¾ ton pickup truck with their big beer belly hanging over their belt, while they bemoan how hard it is to make ends meet. These "poor" people always seem to have plenty to eat and drink.

PEOPLE WHO COMPLAIN ABOUT DOING NORMAL HOUSEHOLD CHORES

I know, it is difficult for people to throw those clothes in the washer and unscrew a cap and pour in the detergent, and then push a button, and leave the machine to do the work while the person goes off to watch television. I realize it is such a burden to get off that couch, put the television show on pause and walk back to put that laundry into another machine adjacent to the first one and then push another button and then walk back to the couch and continue watching television while the dryer does the work.

Come on, people, laundry operations have been modernized for 70 years now. No longer are the days when we have to pump water, scrub the clothes on a wash board, run them through a ringer and then hang them on the clothesline.

My grandmother was a bit old-fashioned and continued to use the clothesline even though she had a dryer. As a young boy, it always gave me a pretty good laugh to park in the driveway at my grandparent's house and see 30 or more pairs of my grandparents' underwear flapping in the wind.

SCOOTERS EVERYWHERE!

I have to admit, I secretly get a chuckle when one of these obnoxious scooter riders bite the dust on the city sidewalk. The sidewalks are supposed to be for pedestrians. But… I must watch out for people flying past me at 20 miles an hour on the sidewalk. These people aren't riding these to save the environment. This is simply the latest fad for people who have time to goof around. These people are too busy to walk amongst their fellow human beings. To further prove their self-importance, they leave the scooters parked right in front of doors, handicap ramps, and the middle of the sidewalk when they are finished with them.

People who brag about and clamor to get the latest cell phone

When did someone's cell phone become such a fashion statement? I mean it is just a phone that allows the owner to call another person. It's not new technology. Why the need for an updated phone each 12 months? What could they possibly upgrade? A cell phone already responds in split seconds. How much faster does it need to be? I often see lines of people stacked up at the phone store when the new model comes out just so they can say they have the latest model. Can people be any shallower?

CONCLUSION

Thank you for listening to me get this all off my chest. I am sure that a lot of people will probably think that I am a crotchety old Grinch. Some people will be able to relate to my commentary.

I really hope it gives a few of you a chuckle, while at the same time reassures you that you are not the only one who feels alienated by our current culture.

Hopefully, some of the items mentioned have caused some self-reflection.

For any millennials who have been offended, please call your local college campus to locate the nearest safe space that offers coloring books, cookies, and play dough.

ABOUT THE AUTHOR

Thomas E. "Tom" Gray was born in Oklahoma City in 1972. Tom grew up in a conservative family and social environment. Tom graduated from Oklahoma State University in 1995 with a bachelor's degree in Agricultural Economics. He currently resides in Texas.